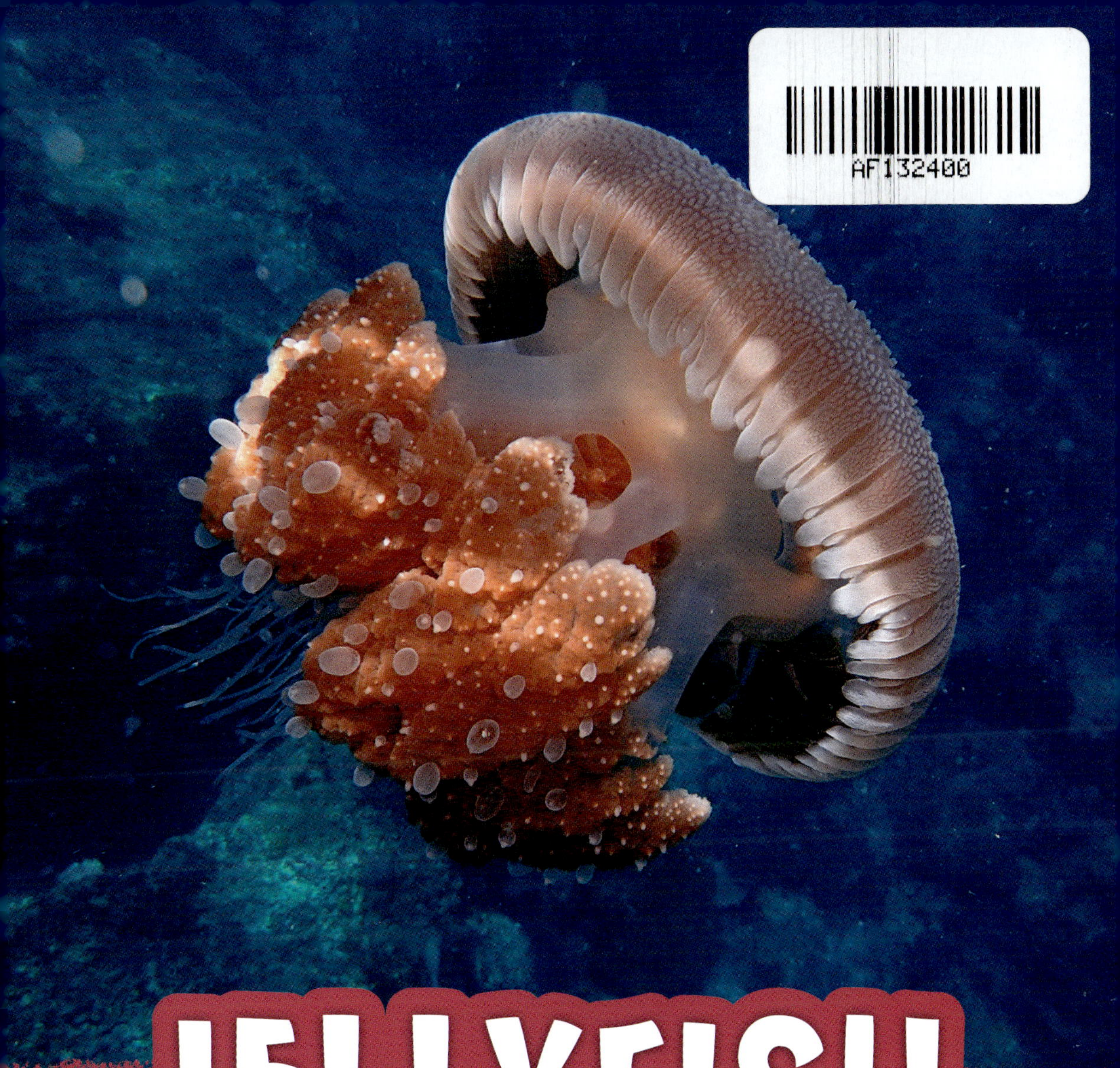

JELLYFISH

by Jaclyn Jaycox

raintree
a Capstone company — publishers for children

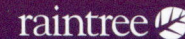

Raintree is an imprint of Capstone Global Library Limited, a company incorporated in England and Wales having its registered office at 264 Banbury Road, Oxford, OX2 7DY – Registered company number: 6695582

www.raintree.co.uk
myorders@raintree.co.uk

Hardback edition text © Capstone Global Library Limited 2023
Paperback edition text © Capstone Global Library Limited 2024

The moral rights of the proprietor have been asserted. All rights reserved. No part of this publication may be reproduced in any form or by any means (including photocopying or storing it in any medium by electronic means and whether or not transiently or incidentally to some other use of this publication) without the written permission of the copyright owner, except in accordance with the provisions of the Copyright, Designs and Patents Act 1988 or under the terms of a licence issued by the Copyright Licensing Agency, 5th Floor, Shackleton House, 4 Battle Bridge Lane, London, SE1 2HX (www.cla.co.uk). Applications for the copyright owner's written permission should be addressed to the publisher.

ISBN 978 1 3982 3879 4 (hardback)
ISBN 978 1 3982 3880 0 (paperback)

Image Credits
Alamy: Blue Planet Archive, 25; Newscom: MEGA/Dan Abbott, 10, picture alliance/blickwinkel/F, 23, VWPics/Andre Seale, 22; Science Source: ANT Photo Library, 15, Robert C. Hermes, 17, 18, Rubén Duro, 24; Shutterstock: Damsea, 5, 8, 14, Hasanul Fahad C A, 1, 7, InkheartX, 27, J.R. Sosky, 21, Paul Gallagher, 9, Peter Gudella, 13, Rich Carey, 26, silvergull, Cover, SunflowerMomma, 11, WorldStock, 28

Editorial Credits
Editors: Gena Chester and Abby Huff; Designer: Dina Her;
Media Researcher: Jo Miller; Production Specialist: Tori Abraham

All internet sites appearing in back matter were available and accurate when this book was sent to press.

British Library Cataloguing in Publication Data
A full catalogue record for this book is available from the British Library.

Contents

Amazing jellyfish 4

Where in the world 6

Jellyfish bodies 10

On the menu 16

Life of a jellyfish 20

Dangers to jellyfish 26

    Fast facts 29

    Glossary 30

    Find out more 31

    Index 32

Words in **bold** are in the glossary.

Amazing jellyfish

A strange animal floats in the sea. It looks like an umbrella with strings hanging down. What could it be? It's a jellyfish!

Jellyfish are not really fish. They are **invertebrates**. They have no backbones. There are more than 2,000 types. But scientists think there may be thousands more. They just haven't been found yet.

mauve stinger

Where in the world

Jellyfish live all around the world. They are found in every ocean. Some live in icy Arctic waters. Others live in warm tropical waters.

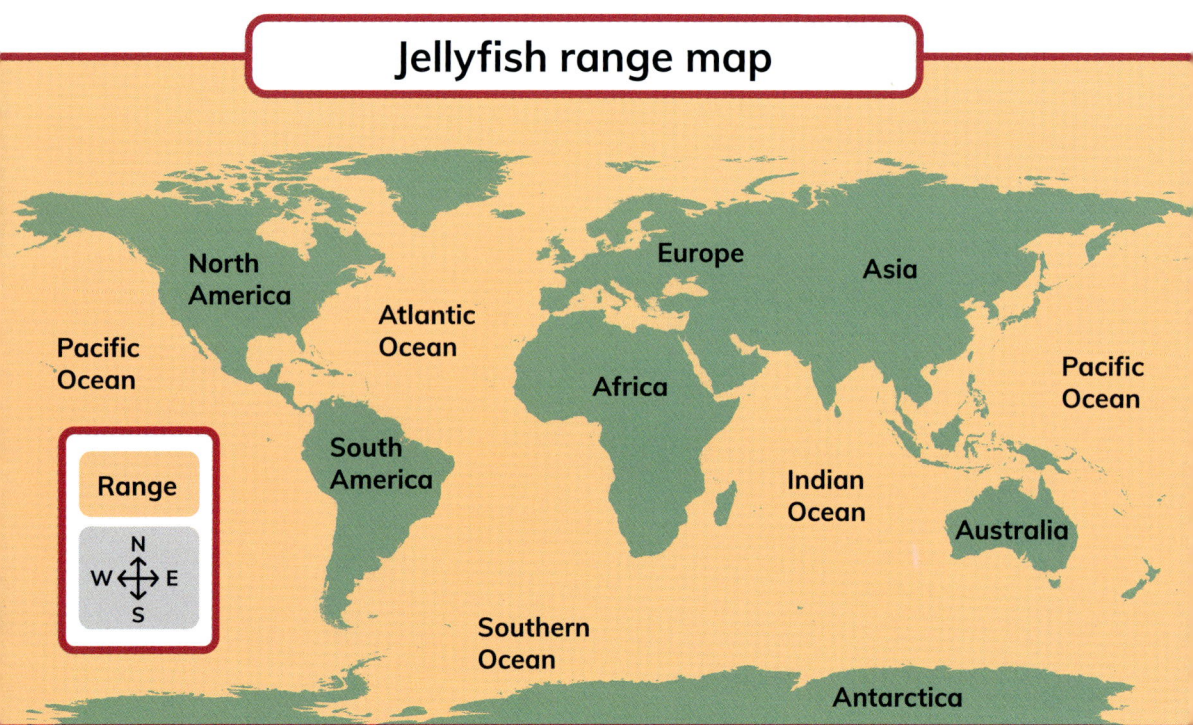

A jellyfish swims near the ocean floor.

Jellyfish can be found near the shore. Or they can be in the middle of the ocean. Some stay by the ocean floor. Others swim near the water's surface.

many-ribbed jellyfish

Jellyfish have been around for millions of years. They existed before the dinosaurs! They can live in many temperatures. They live in different types of water too. This has helped them to survive for so long.

To swim, jellyfish suck in water. Then they quickly push it out. This moves them forward. But they only go a short way. So, they often float in ocean **currents**. This is how they get around and find food.

compass jellyfish

Jellyfish bodies

Jellyfish come in many sizes. The smallest is about the size of a pinhead. The largest ever seen was almost 36.6 metres (120 feet) long. That is longer than three school buses!

barrel jellyfish

crystal jellyfish

Jellyfish are made up of 95 per cent water. Their bodies are soft and jellylike. Some are clear. Others are pink, yellow and blue. They come in other colours too. Some even glow.

Jellyfish are not like most animals. They don't have bones or blood. They don't have a heart or a brain. Instead, their bodies have a **nerve net**. The nerves sense changes in the water. This lets the jellyfish know if food or **predators** are near.

Some jellyfish have eye-like parts. But they don't see in the way human eyes do. Most only sense light.

moon jellyfish

Jellyfish have a main body. It is called the bell. Parts called **tentacles** hang down from the bell. They can be long or short. They can sting. A poison shoots out of the tentacles. The sting keeps **predators** away.

Jellyfish stings can hurt humans. The stings can be painful. Some are very dangerous. A box jellyfish is one of the most poisonous animals in the world. Its sting can kill a human in minutes.

box jellyfish

On the menu

Jellyfish are not picky. They will eat almost anything that fits in their mouths. Small jellyfish eat tiny plants and animals called **plankton**. Large jellyfish eat fish, shrimp and crabs. Some make a meal of other jellyfish!

Many jellyfish catch **prey** with their tentacles. Their sting makes prey unable to move. Then the jellyfish gobbles up its food!

Jellyfish digest food in their stomachs inside their bells.

A jellyfish **digests** its food very fast. This makes it easier for it to float. The food moves from its mouth to its stomach. The food gets broken down quickly.

Like with people, this process makes waste. Water runs through the jellyfish. It pushes the waste back out of the mouth.

Life of a jellyfish

Some types of jellyfish live alone. Others live in groups. These groups are called swarms, smacks or blooms. A swarm can have thousands of jellyfish. Some even have millions! Scientists think there are different reasons they get together in groups. They might gather where there is lots of food.

Another reason jellyfish gather is to **mate**. Females let their eggs out into the water. The eggs float around. They stick to a hard surface, such as a rock. The eggs turn into **polyps**.

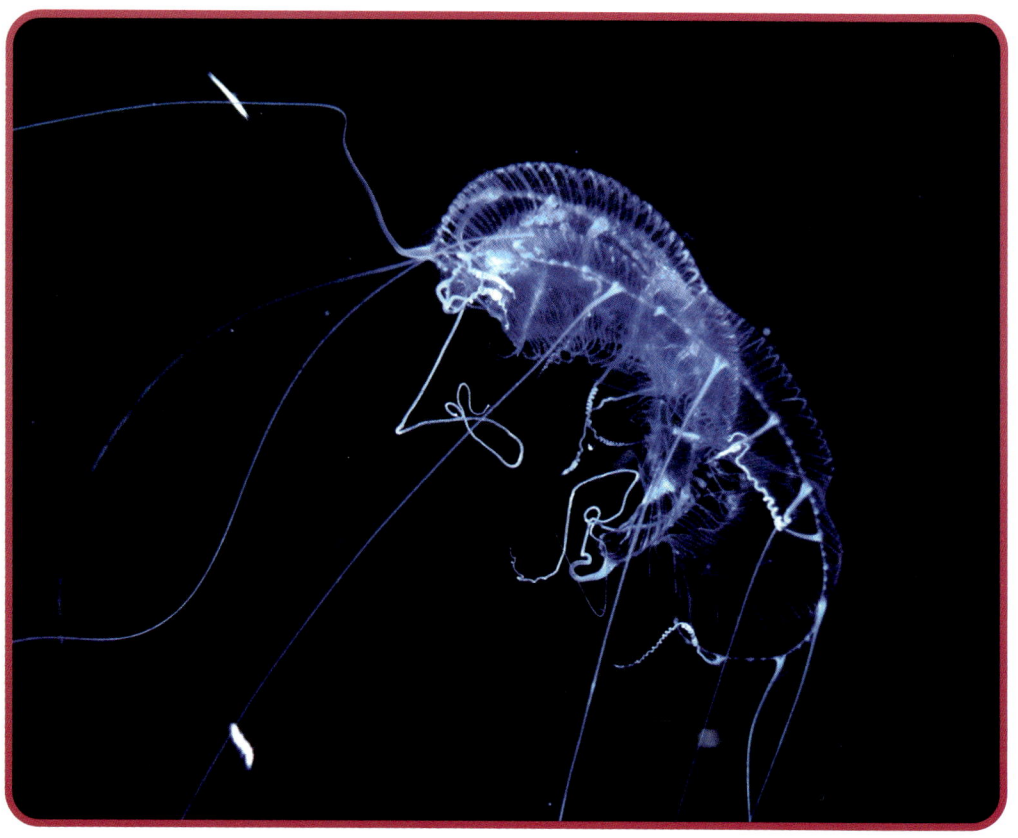

polyps

A polyp looks like a small tube. At the end is a mouth. Around the mouth are small tentacles. These grab food. The polyp eats tiny sea animals.

A young jellyfish starts to break from a polyp.

The polyp grows. Many small jellyfish start to bud from it. The jellyfish break free. They float in the ocean. They eat and grow. They become adults when they are ready to mate.

Most jellyfish live for less than one year. But some types live only for a few hours. Others live for up to 30 years. One type may be able to live forever!

Scientists think the immortal jellyfish may never die of old age.

Dangers to jellyfish

A jellyfish's sting helps to keep it safe. But they still have predators. Sea turtles eat them. A turtle's mouth and throat can't be stung. Ocean sunfish also eat jellyfish. Sunfish eyes are set back from their mouths. Jellyfish tentacles can't reach them.

Whales and sharks also hunt jellyfish. In some parts of the world, humans eat them too.

    Jellyfish are not in danger of dying out. In fact, their numbers are getting bigger. This can cause problems. Jellyfish swarms can kill many fish and sea animals. They may gather where people swim. People are more likely to get stung. People are working to keep jellyfish numbers under control.

Fast facts

Name: jellyfish

Habitat: oceans

Where in the world: every ocean on Earth

Food: plankton, fish, shrimp, crabs, other jellyfish

Predators: sea turtles, fish, whales, sharks, other jellyfish, humans

Life span: most live less than one year, but some live for only hours and some may live forever

Glossary

current the movement of water

digest to break down food so it can be used by the body

invertebrate an animal without a backbone

mate when males and females come together to produce young

nerve net fibres in a body that send messages to body parts and control how they move

plankton tiny plants and animals that live in the water and drift with currents

polyp a small sea animal with a tube-like body and a round mouth surrounded by tentacles

predator an animal that hunts other animals for food

prey an animal hunted by another animal for food

tentacle a long, arm-like body part some animals use to feel, grab or smell

Find out more

Books

Deadly Predators (Engineered by Nature), Louise Spilsbury (Raintree, 2020)

Look Inside Seas and Oceans, Megan Cullis (Usborne, 2019)

Marine Habitats Around the World (Exploring Earth's Habitats), Phillip Simpson (Raintree, 2020)

Websites

DK FindOut!: Jellyfish
www.dkfindout.com/uk/animals-and-nature/jellyfish-corals-and-anemones/jellyfish/

National Geographic Kids: Jellyfish facts
www.natgeokids.com/uk/discover/animals/sea-life/jellyfish-facts/

Index

bodies 4, 10, 11, 12, 14, 19

currents 9

digesting 19

eggs 22

humans 12, 15, 19, 27, 28

invertebrates 4

life spans 25

mating 22, 24

nerve nets 12

polyps 22–24

predators 12, 14, 26–27

prey 9, 12, 16, 19, 20, 23

range 6

sizes 10, 16

stinging 14, 15, 16, 26, 28

swarms 20, 28

swimming 7, 9

tentacles 14, 16, 23, 26

types 4, 10, 11, 15, 20, 25

About the author

Jaclyn Jaycox is a children's book author and editor. She lives in southern Minnesota, USA, with her husband, two kids and her pet goldendoodle.